NONE
DARE
CALL
IT
TREASON!
BOOK 4

America's Illustrious State Department! It's Machiavellian Misdeeds!

Robert W. Pelton
$4.95

"Treason doth never prosper,

"What's the reason?

"Why if it prosper,

"None dare call it treason."

John Harrington

Printed in America
On Recycled Paper
In
Charleston, South Carolina

Published in America
By
The Freedom & Liberty
Foundation Press
Knoxville, Tennessee

Dedicated
To
My Beloved
America

The greatest, most generous, most benevolent and most powerful nation on the face of the earth – and the only country in the history of the world to have been founded on Biblical principles.

A nation can survive its fools, and even the ambitious. But it cannot survive treason from within. An enemy at the gates is less formidable, for he is known and he carries his banners openly.

The traitor moves among those within the gates freely, his sly whispers rustling through the galleys, heard in the very hall of government itself.

For the traitor appears not traitor. He speaks in the accent familiar to his victims, and he wears their face and their garments, and he appeals to the baseness that lies deep in the hearts of all men.

He rots the soul of a nation - he works secretly and unknown in the night to undermine the pillars of a city - he infects the body politic so that it can no longer resist.

A murderer is less to be feared.

Cicero, 42 B.C.

CONTENTS

Forward

Independence Hall Where the Declaration of Independence Was Signed.

Our glorious Declaration of Independence is a timeless divinely inspired masterpiece given to mankind through the anointed pen of Thomas Jefferson.

The grand and unmatched United States Constitution is indisputably the product of Providential guidance and

13

wisdom and certainly not a document which evokes whimsical interpretations with the changing political climates.

All Americans have a moral obligation to stand up and be counted in these trying times!

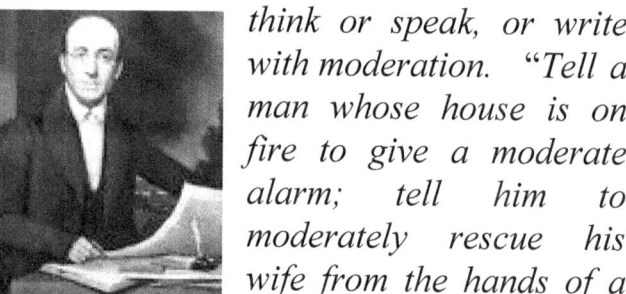

Abraham Lincoln boldly declared: *"To sin by silence when they should protest, makes cowards of men."*

William Lloyd Garrison capsulized it best: *"As a free man who is determined to remain free -- I do not wish to think or speak, or write with moderation. "Tell a man whose house is on fire to give a moderate alarm; tell him to moderately rescue his wife from the hands of a ravisher; tell the mother to gradually extricate her babe from the fire into which it has fallen -- but urge me not to use moderation in a course like the present."*

Senator Barry Goldwater, 1964 Presidential candidate was castigated and verbally crucified by the media.

14

He simply stated this simple truism: *"Extremism in the pursuit of Liberty is no vice."*

This good and moral man of character soundly rocked the boat of the propagandists. He was as a result soundly defeated in the election.

The alarmed media wolves panicked the voters with their jeers and sneers and insane howls about this man's lack of *"moderation!"*

It can honestly be said that through the Providential genius of our Founding Fathers, the remaining remnants of the original American Constitutional Republic still provides more freedom, opportunity and abundance for mankind than is found in any other nation in the world.

This is true despite decade after decade of unabated treason and treachery promulgated by innumerable traitorous individuals found buried in the twiddle dee – twiddle dum administrations of both the Democrats and the Republicans.

An informed and active, not a media brainwashed electorate, is the only antidote to further prostitution of, and the ultimate destruction of, what Benjamin Franklin called our Republic.

Preface

"Treason against the United States shall consist only in levying war against them, or in adhering to their enemies, giving them aid and comfort."

U.S. Constitution. Article 111, Section 3

What is your treason I.Q.?

If you can answer the following questions, it's high.

If you miss one or more, you should read the *None Dare Call It Treason* series!

Who was behind allowing Red Chinese soldiers take airborne training at Fort Benning, Georgia?

Is this not treason?

Why was South Vietnam, South Africa, Rhodesia and numerous other American friends deliberately betrayed to the forces of evil?

Is this not treason?

Why was our friend Chiang Kai Shek not so gently coerced into a Communist dictatorship by highly placed subversives in the State Department?

Is this not treason?

Why was Cuba treasonously delivered into the clutches of Communist revolutionary Fidel Castro?

Is this not treason?

Why have untold millions of dollars consistently been used to prop up faltering Red dictatorships and to assist Communist terrorists in overthrowing non-Communist governments?

Is this not treason?

What American company sold nuclear reactors to Communist Occupied Romania?

Is this not treason?

Name the company that provided Communist Hungary with a factory designed to make 1.5 million light bulbs daily?

Is this not treason?

What well known oil company invested $1 billion for oil exploration in Communist Occupied Angola?

Is this not treason?

Can you name the American company who treasonously built and equipped a $10 million electronics plant near Warsaw for the Polish slave labor tyranny?

Is this not treason?

These are questions to which every American should rightfully have an honest answer.

Unfortunately most do not!

Tragedy was carefully orchestrated by traitors in our Government and the media with regard to Cuba, Vietnam, Laos, Cambodia, Rhodesia, China, El Salvador, Nicaragua and many other countries.

Anastasio Somoza was the former President of free Nicaragua.

He offered this startling insight in his 1980 book, Nicaragua Betrayed: *"I have factual evidence that the betrayal of Nicaragua was not perpetrated out of ignorance, but rather by design."*

Somoza was soon after assassinated!

Is this not treason?

John Lehman, Secretary of the Navy, made this shocking statement on May 25 to the 1983 Annapolis graduating class: *"Within weeks many of you will be looking across just hundreds of feet of water at some of the most modern technology ever invented in America.*

"Unfortunately, it is on Soviet ships."

Is this not treason?

Earl E.T. Smith was the American Ambassador to Cuba when it was similarly delivered to the Communists.

He makes this concise comment on July 14, 1986: *"Nicaragua is Cuba all over again."*

Can you name the company that paid the Communist dictatorship in Angola over $600 million annually in taxes and oil royalties.

This money bought new Soviet jets, tanks and helicopter gunships.

And it paid Castro for supplying 35,000 imported Cuban mercenaries who keep the Angolan people enslaved.

Is this not treason?

Stressed retired Brigadier General Andrew J. Gatsis on August 11, 1986: *"Though aware of the Communist goal of world domination, the average U.S. Citizen refuses to believe that the real threat comes from governmental officials and their non-*  *governmental confederates who secretly espouse the same objectives as the openly avowed Communists."*

Anthony Sutton stated in his 1986 book *The Best Enemy Money Can Buy: "We now have the formidable task of bringing these gentlemen to the bar of justice to publicly answer for their private and concealed actions."*

The *None Dare Call It Treason* series certainly won't win accolades from the United Nations or the State Department!

Nor will Harvard feel compelled to bestow an honorary degree upon the author!

Harvard Law School was the spawning ground for an incredible number of Red agents. Included were members of the first Soviet spy ring ever to be exposed in our government.

Reed Irvine aptly commented in July of 1986: *"Indeed, it has long been a joke among refugees from Eastern Europe that there are more Marxists at Harvard than there are in the Soviet Union, or Poland, or whatever Communist country the refugee called home."*

The Honorable Ezra Taft Benson said: *"The truth must be told even at the risk of destroying, in large measure, the influence of men who are widely respected and loved by the American people.*

"The stakes are high. Freedom and survival is the issue."

Treason is still a most serious federal offense.

The *None Dare Call It Treason* series examines the reasons for and the Americans behind the fall of freedom and the rise of tyranny throughout the world!

Has anything really changed?
You Decide!

Treason

Whoever, owing allegiance to the United States, levies war against them or adheres to their enemies, giving them aid and comfort within the United States or elsewhere, is guilty of treason and shall suffer death, or be imprisoned not less than five years and fined not less than $10,000; and shall be incapable of holding any office under the United states.

U.S. Code, Title 18, Section 2381

Whoever, owing allegiance to the United States and having knowledge of the commission of any treason against them, conceals and does not, as soon as may be, disclose and make known the same to the President or to some judge of the United States, or to the Governor or to some judge or justice of a particular state, is guilty of misprision of treason, and shall be fined not more than $1000 or imprisoned not more than 7 years or both.   *U.S. Code, Title 18, Section 2382*

America's Illustrious State Department!

It's Machiavellian Misdeeds!

Treason: *"The betrayal of one's country, esp. by giving aid to an enemy."*

The American Heritage Dictionary

"The 'Liberals' ask what proof we have that Communists have been, and are influencing the policies of our government?"* offers the Honorable Martin Dies, former Chairman of the  House Committee on Un-American Activities. *"Our answer is: all the proof it was possible to obtain under hostile Administrations which actively smeared and persecuted every Committee of Congress which has tried to get the facts.*

"No 'Liberal' will tell us what the eight hundred [actually 858] security risks named by Scott McLeod in 1956 are doing even now in our State Department, unless they are surrendering us to the Reds."

Consider the years when Alger Hiss and his Communist cronies were running the show!

How many more Red moles were Hiss and others of like ideology instrumental in bringing into the Foreign Service and elsewhere in government?

The heirs of Hiss certainly didn't quit when their mentor, benefactor, and idol was imprisoned in 1950.

He'd been tried and found guilty of lying to a Grand Jury about being an espionage agent for Communist Occupied Russia!

Hiss participated in a cornucopia of traitorous acts and treasonous deeds.

Yet he was prosecuted *only* for being a liar while under oath,

He was *not* prosecuted or being a traitor!

Why?

We must carefully examine the State Department's past and present track record.

When for example has the State Department done anything resulting in something beneficial for the United States in foreign policy?

Or rather, when has the State Department done anything not favoring the global designs of America's dire enemies?

Look at the State Department's traitorous machinations with regard to:

Hungary
Cuba
the Congo
Yugoslavia
Nicaragua

And the rest of the Communist occupied slave labor dictatorships!

Look at the State Department's traitorous machinations with regard to:

South Africa
Taiwan
South Vietnam
Laos
Rhodesia

And other anti-Communist American allies as well!

All were betrayed to the forces of evil by conspirators in the United States government!

When was the last time Communist penetration of the State Department was investigated?

President Dwight D. Eisenhower promised during his Presidential campaigns to *"clean out"* the agency!

President Richard Milhous Nixon promised the same thing.

Neither did anything of the sort!

Nor did they really intend to!

Even during the Reagan years the arrogant subversives in the State Department and elsewhere in the government were still untouchable entities!

They insolently ran foreign policy!

Contrary to the President's proclaimed goals.

And contrary to the best interests of America.

This is especially appalling when anyone reads the *United States Government Organizational Manual*.

According to this the State Department's primary objective is supposed to  be *"to promote the long-range security and well-being of the United States."*

Some years ago highly placed Kremlin moles in the State Department deliberately undermined and brought down the government of Nationalist China!

President Harry S. Truman enthusiastically supported the betrayal of Chiang Kai-shek.

Yes!

This sell out took place despite the fact that the Chinese leader had long been a dependable friend of the U.S.

The country was treasonously relinquished to Mao's Red Chinese gangsters in 1949.

Free China was not so gently coerced into a Communist dictatorship -- one of the bloodiest tyrannies the world has ever known!

The Red terrorists looted the country.

They established their police state.

They orchestrated an unceasing murder spree.

And they proceeded to decimate the population.

 Chiang Kai-shek's Nationalist Army was close to total victory over Mao's Communist guerrilla forces near the end of 1945.

Truman rushed General George Catlett Marshall, a close friend of Eisenhower, over to China.

It was supposedly an effort to stop the rout of the Reds!

Marshall gained a malodorous reputation in the Truman Administration.

He was the official most responsible for Free China's betrayal to the Communists.

Chiang Kai-shek had been clearly winning the war.

Yet he was forced by Marshall to agree to a cease fire.

He balked at surrendering to the very Communist guerrillas he was so soundly defeating.

The United States was supposedly helping Nationalist China.

How?

By sending Chiang Kai-shek hundreds of millions of dollars worth of war goods.

The anti-Communist forces desperately needed small arms and ammunition.

So entrenched were Communists in the State Department that Chiang got nothing of value!

His supply depots were turned into military junkyards.

According to Colonel L.B. Moody who was there at the time Chiang Kai-shek's anti-Communist forces got *"billions of moldy cigarettes, blown up guns and junk bombs, and disabled vehicles from the Pacific islands."*

America's free Chinese friends received machine guns with missing tripods! Tanks with spiked guns! Rifles with no ammunition clips!

And planes with no fuel!

Furthermore explained Freda Utley: *"President Truman took steps to prevent the National forces from obtaining arms and ammunition.*

"On August 14, 1946, President Truman issued an executive order saying that China was not to be allowed to acquire any 'surplus' American weapons 'which could be used in fighting a civil war,' meaning a war with the Communists."

George Marshall as Secretary of State boasted: *"As Chief-of-Staff I armed 39 anti-Communist divisions.*

"Now with a stroke of a pen I disarm them."

Marshall clearly knew what he was doing!

The *Sell-Out-China Program* went exactly as scripted by the multitude of Red moles who were deeply imbedded in the State Department.

Ambassador William D. Pawley agreed.

He blamed the tragic loss of China on the

subversive machinations of Kremlin agents and pro-Communists solidly entrenched throughout the State Department.

Included were notable subversives including:

Owen Lattimore
John Stewart Service
Philip Jessup
John Paton Davies Jr.
John Carter Vincent
Dean Acheson
O. Edmund Clubb.

A few more of the conspirators devoted to delivering China to the Reds were Communists:

Agnes Smedley
Frederick Vanderbilt Field
Alger Hiss
Maxwell Stewart
Lauchlin Currie.

John Stewart Service was in June 1945 recalled to Washington.

This was done at the insistence of the

Ambassador to China.

All of the above named individuals were either working for the State Department. Or for the Institute of Pacific Relations.

This particular group was cited as being controlled by *"a small core of officials and staff members"* who *"were either Communist or pro-Communist."*

Ambassador Pawley was asked if the Red takeover of the Chinese mainland could possibly have been the result of *"sincere mistakes of judgment."*

His unequivocal reply: *"No, I don't."*

General Wedemeyer for whom John Stewart Service worked charged the man with supporting the murderous Chinese Communist forces!

Patrick Hurley accused Service of passing secret information to the Reds!

Reports written by Service, John Carter Vincent, John Paton Davies and many other conspirators never deviated from the Party line.

Designed to discredit Hurley these propaganda reports were regularly sent to Washington without the Ambassador ever having seen them!

A total of eleven leftist advisors were finally unloaded by Hurley.

They included:

George Acheson, Jr.
Raymond P. Ludden
Fulton Freeman
Edward E. Rice
Philip D. Sprouse
Hungerford B. Howard.

Hurley was shortly thereafter brought before the Chinese Affairs Board of the State Department.

He explained: *"I was called on the carpet, with a full array of the pro-Communists of the State Department as my judge and questioners."*

Ambassador Hurley resigned in disgust during November of 1945 after learning that all the traitors he'd fired had instead been promoted.

Most of these subversives were now his bosses!

Identified Communist John Carter Vincent became a division head!

Arthur Ringwalt became acting chief of the China Division!

Two other security risks became Ringwalt's assistants.

John Paton Davies was identified as a Communist by Hurley.

This traitor was retained as a member of Dean Acheson's policy planning staff!

He was later transferred to the Moscow embassy with another China conspirator named Horace Smith.

John Stewart Service was assigned to General MacArthur's staff.

To his credit MacArthur refused to accept the traitor.

Immediately following the takeover of China in 1949 Mao Tse-tung and his Communist thugs orchestrated a massive orgy of death and destruction.

They had the assistance of multiple traitors in the U.S. government.

Approximately 64 million unarmed Chinese civilians were methodically slaughtered!

Time reported: *"These are figures that stagger the imagination.*

"In no previous war, revolution or human holocaust have so many people been destroyed in so short a period."

Professor Richard L. Walker was a foremost China scholar.

He explained how Moscow-trained Mao and his vengeful comrades handled things after gaining power: *"Many of the executions took place after mass public trials in which the assembled crowds, whipped up to a frenzy by planted agitators, called invariably for the death penalty and for no mercy for the accused.*

"Mao and colleagues made no effort to conceal the violent course being followed.

"On the contrary, the most gruesome and detailed accounts were printed in the Communist press and broadcast over the official radio for the purpose of amplifying the condition of mass terror the trials were clearly intended to induce."

Mao's highly touted *Great Leap Forward* from 1958 to 1960 was directly responsible for an incredible 27 million more murders!

Amnesty International cites recent evidence of a continuing policy of "*mass executions.*"

Comrade Wang-Jingrong matter-of-factly brushes it all off: *"We have a population of 1 billion and those executed only comprise a small number comparatively!"*

Missionary Raymond J. DeJaegher told of a typical atrocity committed by Communist Chinese gangsters in Ping Shan.

Those who participated thoroughly enjoyed their sadistic task: *"The son was held and forced to watch the awful process and listen to his father's screams of agony.*

"The Reds poured vinegar and acids over the man's body so that the skin would come off quickly and make the job a quick and easy one.

"He began at the back, peeling from the shoulders down in long strips.

"The man was skinned entirely, except for his head.

"He died within a few minutes after the peeler had completed his gruesome task."

DeJaegher recalled how Communist Chinese soldiers brought 13 prisoners to a school playground.

The teachers and their students were called outside to observe.

The tightly bound men were forced to kneel.

False accusations were made!

The school children were told to sing patriotic songs.

All 13 captives were quickly decapitated.

DeJaegher described it this way: *"Several among the group rushed forward and pushed the corpses over on their backs.*

"Each soldier bent down with a sharp knife and made a quick, circular incision in the chest.

"He then jumped on the abdomen with both feet, or pumped on it over and over with one foot, forcing the heart out of the incision.

"Then he swooped down again, snipped and plucked it out.

When they had collected the thirteen hearts they strung them all on a pointed marsh reed which they tied together to make a carrying device."

The Red Chinese were totally ruthless in dealing with unwanted segments of their society.

Reverend Shih-ping Wang revealed one aspect of the horror: *"All the elderly people 60 years of age and above who cannot work are put in the old people's 'Happy Home'!*

"They are given shots!

"They are told these shots are for their health.

"But after the shots are taken they die within two weeks.

44

"After they die, the corpses are placed in vats.

"When the bodies decay and maggots set in, the maggots are used to feed the chickens!

"The remainder of the body is used for fertilizer!"

Hurley sacrificed his career in an attempt to warn Americans of the powerful Communist influence in the State Department.

He vainly appeared before the Senate Foreign Relations Committee.

His firsthand knowledge of Red penetration and domination was mindlessly ignored.

His testimony was ridiculed and labeled *"absurd"* by the illustrious Senators!

45

Louis Budenz, a former top Party leader, testified: *"The Communists relied very strongly on Service and John Carter Vincent in a campaign against Ambassador Hurley."*

A major push was initiated at this time to drive all anti-Communists out of the State Department.

Budenz revealed that Communist Party members were ordered to force the resignation of anyone *"considered to be against Soviet policy in the Far East."*

Professor Anthony Kubek revealed how anti-Communists, or *"reactionaries"* as they were labeled by the Reds, were methodically

eliminated: *"There was unloosed a barrage of insidious smear attacks and an all-out attempt to discredit the anti-Communists in the Department of State.*

"This was done through Communist front organizations and by those liberal elements of press and radio who customarily promote the key Soviet objectives while pretending to oppose 'Communism.'

"It is interesting to note that in all cases the men singled out by the Communists were removed.

"In effect, the hiring and firing of our State Department personnel was done in Moscow!"

In this way the Dean Acheson clique replaced anti-Communists with Communists and pro-Communists in all strategic State Department positions.

Acheson was well rewarded as a result of his unwavering leftist policies.

He became President Truman's Secretary of State from 1949 to 1953.

Here Acheson helped hide the Communist background of Alger Hiss!

He pushed Moscow's man up through the ranks, all the while knowing that Hiss was a spy taking orders directly from the Kremlin!

Again consider the words of Joseph Stalin: *"Some are members of the party, some are not; but that is a formal difference.*

"The important thing is that both serve the same common purpose."

Should this not tell us something?

47

The Voice of America began broadcasting programs about *"freeing the captive peoples"* and *"rolling back the iron curtain."*

The people of Communist Occupied Hungary were led to believe the United States would come to their aid if there were to be an uprising!

As a result, they bravely revolted in October 1956 and drove out their Soviet masters!

Even the Russian troops in Budapest turned on the Communist leadership and joined the freedom fighters!

 Imre Nagy's newly formed anti-Communist government pleaded with the State Department for diplomatic recognition.

The pleas of the heroic Freedom Fighters were ignored!

 What would have happened had the United States come through with the promised assistance?

Soviet defector Oleg Penkovsky was in Moscow at the time.

He explained: *"We in Moscow felt as if we were sitting on a powderkeg.*

"Everyone in the General Staff was against the 'Khrushchev adventure.'

"It was better to lose Hungary, as they said, than to lose everything.

"But what did the West do?

"Nothing!

"It was asleep.

"This gave Khrushchev confidence.

"If the West had slapped Khrushchev down hard then all of Eastern Europe could be free."

On November 2, 1956 President Eisenhower completed the betrayal of Hungary's captive people!

A treasonous State Department cablegram was sent to Tito, Yugoslavia's Communist dictator.

It read: *"The government of the United States does not look with favor upon governments unfriendly to the Soviet Union on the borders of the Soviet Union."*

This was the death knell for the Hungarian Freedom Fighters!

The State Department had given its tacit approval for the Soviet tanks massed on the Hungarian border to invade.

They did exactly that just 36 hours later!

On November 4 Nikita Khrushchev afterwards known as *"the Butcher of Budapest"* used thousands of savages brought in from Mongolia.

These barbarians easily crushed the uprising!

On this sad day, the Hungarian Freedom Fighters broadcast their final words: *"People of the world, listen to our call.*

"Help us not with words, but with action, with soldiers and arms.

"Please do not forget that this wild attack of Bolshevism will not stop.

"You may be the next victim.

"Save us.

"Our ship is sinking.

"The light vanishes.

"The shadows grow darker from hour to hour.

"Listen to our cry.

"Start moving.

"Extend to us your brotherly hands.

"God be with you and us."

The Freedom Fighters would wait in vain for the Americans to come!

The incredible State Department treachery resulted in over 15,000 casualties in Budapest alone.

Was this travesty no more than a series of mistakes in judgment?

Not hardly!

It was planned that way!

The Eisenhower State Department obviously meant for Hungary's anti-Communist revolt to fail!

In December of 1958, Senator Thomas Dodd said this: *"What many people*

had considered impossible came to pass.

"While we stood by in confusion and disarray and apparent helplessness, a Communist dictator was installed on the island of Cuba, only 90 miles off our own shores."

Consider carefully the implications of Dodd's words in reference to this portion of the 1956 House study entitled *Soviet Total War: "Communist strategy teaches that there can be no successful revolution followed by the creation of Soviets in any Latin American country unless an internal revolution has been effected within the United States.*

"The Comintern views the Western hemisphere as an integral unit in which the United States must first be rendered helpless before a Soviet-type government can be established in any other of the 20 republics in the   hemisphere."

Shockingly enough this study was issued more than two years prior to Castro and his gangster group coming to power in Cuba.

It was ignored by everyone in government!

It was ignored by the media!

The Communist's own game plan tells us they couldn't install a Castro in Cuba.

An Ortega in Nicaragua.

Or a Red dictator anywhere else in our hemisphere *"unless an internal revolution has been effected within the United States"* and *"the United States must first be rendered helpless."*

Had there been an internal revolution in the United States?

Had the U.S. government been rendered helpless?

Neither Fidel Castro nor Daniel Ortega could possibly have brought Communism to Cuba or to Nicaragua without the aid, assistance and direction of certain  Communist and pro-Communist elements in the State Department.

And those in the media.

Robert Hill was a former Ambassador to Mexico.

He testified before the Senate Judiciary Committee.

Hill accurately charged that the State Department working hand-in-hand with the *New York Times* delivered Cuba to the Communists!

Earl E.T. Smith was the U.S. Ambassador to Cuba during the Kremlin supported Communist revolution.

He made some serious charges: *"Castro could not have seized power in Cuba without the aid of the United States.*

"American government agencies and the American media played a major role in bringing Castro to power.

"The State Department consistently intervened to bring about the downfall of President Fulgencio Batista, thereby making it possible for Fidel Castro to take over the government of Cuba."

Security risk William Arthur Wieland was one of the subversive super stars in the game of *Deliver Cuba to Communist Occupied Russia*!

He obtained his job without a security check!

And without even filling out an application!

The SISS report reveals some pertinent facts about his background: *"Before joining the Foreign Service during World War II Wieland lived in Cuba under the alias 'Arturo Montenegro'.*

"Wieland entered the Foreign Service when its Latin American Department was headed by a Soviet agent, Lawrence Duggan."

Duggan (CFR) was a close pal of broadcaster Edward R. Murrow.

He was exposed as having *"collaborated with agents of the Soviet intelligence apparatus."*

This Communist spy was scheduled to testify before a Congressional investigating committee in 1948.

But his life ended rather abruptly!

He conveniently *"fell"* from a Manhattan hotel window.

Not so strangely, many Communists have fatal *"accidents"* when their reliability becomes questionable.

Kremlin spy Harry Dexter White's life also ended suddenly.

He had a mysterious fatal heart attack under similar circumstances!

The SISS findings continue: *"As a reported 'protégé' of Sumner Welles, Wieland 'earned' four promotions in nine months and was assigned to Brazil in 1947 as press attaché."*

 The American Ambassador to Brazil William Pawley informed Eisenhower as well as State Department officials of Wieland's leftist activities.

His warnings were ignored!

Wieland was again promoted and sent to Bogata, Columbia.

While vice counsel in Bogota in 1948 Wieland was known to be one of the State Department untouchables.

He openly and defiantly continued his blatant pro-Communist endeavors.

In May of 1957, career diplomat Wieland was *in charge* of the important Caribbean Desk.

This security risk brazenly did pretty much as he pleased to deliver Cuba into the clutches of Communist revolutionary Fidel Castro.

According to the SISS: *"From the time of his appointment to the key State Department post in May 1957, Wieland regularly disregarded, sidetracked or denounced FBI, State Department, and Military Intelligence sources which branded Castro a Communist and showed that his associates were Moscow-trained."*

In August 1959 Wieland wrecked an intelligence briefing given to Dr. Milton Eisenhower by the American Embassy staff in Mexico City.

This just happened to be when it became obvious they were going to prove Castro *was* a Communist.

Wieland was denounced as *"either a damn fool or a Communist'."*

Eisenhower ignored the incident.

This is the same radical leftist who was the President of Johns Hopkins University.

While in this influential position he recommended that a plan be prepared for the gradual surrender of the United States to the Communists!

Yes Milton Eisenhower actually said this!

And remember, this man was the brother of President Dwight D. Eisenhower!

The track record of American foreign policy clearly indicates that this has unquestionably been done!

The SISS notes that Wieland *"never told his superiors officially or wrote in any Department paper what he told friends as early as 1958 or earlier -- that Castro 'is a Communist' and is surrounded by Commies."*

With Wieland's conscious assistance Fidel Castro became Cuba's Red dictator on February 16, 1959.

The SISS concluded: *"Wieland is considered author of the fatal arms embargo which cut off munitions shipments to the anti-Communist Batista while Castro was being liberally supplied by sources in Florida and by Russian submarines surfacing off the Cuban coast.*

"Similar State Department action ten years earlier had crippled Chiang Kai-shek's Army and permitted the Communists to come to power in China."

Pawley wrote: *"The deliberate overthrow of Batista by Wieland and Matthews, assisted by Rubottom, is almost as great a tragedy as the surrendering of China to the Communists by a similar group of Department of State officials."*

Wieland was given a security clearance by *"higher authority"* when John F. Kennedy assumed the Presidency.

The *"higher authority"* was none other than the traitorous Secretary of State Dean Rusk!

Wieland was again promoted!

His new job was to *revise* State Department security procedures!

Kennedy was challenged over Wieland's questionable appointment to such a sensitive position.

Reporter Sarah McLendon rightfully charged that the man was a dangerous security risk!

The President responded by sternly rebuking McLendon.

And not the subversive in question!

He *personally* vouched for Wieland's loyalty.

President Kennedy informed the press that both he and Rusk *(himself a dangerous security risk)* had checked Wieland's record.

They had determined him to be well qualified for the critical job!

JFK said he *"felt confident"* that Wieland could perform his duties *"without detriment to the interests of the United States."*

The President lied!

His nonsensical response wasn't even questioned!

The gutless reporters who were present or the media clones in general said nothing!

Nixon did exactly the same thing in 1969 with Charles Woodruff Yost!

Yost was another high ranking State Department security risk.

And he was a close friend of Soviet spy Alger Hiss.

William Wieland was denied a security clearance by State Department security chief Otto Otepka.

Otepka was fully aware of Wieland's treasonous role in deliberately bringing Fidel Castro to power while knowing the Cuban terrorist was a Communist.

He'd personally sent him hundreds of intelligence reports revealing Castro's Red background.

Otepka testified: *"Either Wieland did not read them, or if he did read them he deliberately misinterpreted them."*

Wieland was rewarded well for his labors in behalf of the Communists even after his role was exposed!

He was given a plum diplomatic post in Australia.

As so many other notorious anti-American security risks have done, Wieland eventually retired with a sizable pension.

This generous pension was paid by the taxpayers of the very country he deliberately betrayed!

"The disastrous policies pursued, one after another, could not be viewed as mistakes, for if they were only such then by the law of averages we should have done something right once in a while," charged Bryton Barron, who was Chief of the Treaty Section for six of his 26 years in the State Department. *"The perpetrators of disaster, themselves, never termed their acts mistakes: the 1949 White Paper on China openly boasted of a policy that brought the Reds to power in mainland China; and that Department official [Wieland] whose activities helped bring Castro to power was subsequently promoted."*

Dwight D. Eisenhower declared: *"Only a genius and a prophet could have known for sure that Cuban Premier [dictator] Fidel Castro was a Communist in the 1950s."*

Eisenhower was either grossly uninformed or he was a liar!

Many people knew!

For example, in September 1958, prior to the Red takeover of Cuba, Robert Welch declared: *"The evidence from Castro's whole past, that he is a Communist agent carrying out Communist orders and plans is overwhelming."*

Welch was literally crucified by the rabid leftist media!

Why?

He said nothing other than the truth!

That Fidel Castro was a Communist was known at least a decade earlier than this!

According to the SISS, William Arthur Wieland and other subversives knew Castro was a Communist terrorist: *"While the American vice counsel in Bogata, Wieland knew a young Cuban revolutionary.*

"During the riots in 1948 U.S. officials heard him broadcast,

'This is Fidel Castro.

"This is a Communist revolution.'

"Both Wieland and Roy Rubottom, Assistant Secretary of State and Wieland's superior were in Bogota during the riots."

Dr. Fernando Penabaz was a prominent Havana attorney when the Castro terrorists took control of Cuba.

Two men he knew were placed in a small sealed cell.

Penabaz explained: *"They felt that their feet were sinking into something soft.*

"The impression is that you're sinking in dust.

"Almost immediately, you hear a whirring sound of high-powered fans.

"What you have sunk into is not dust; it is ground glass.

"The glass begins to permeate your nose, your ears, your mouth.

"You try desperately to breathe, and then you begin to hemorrhage -- blood from the ears, blood from the nose, blood from the throat."

In 1947, Lieutenant General Albert Wedemeyer was ordered to analyze the volatile Korean situation.

The development of a strong South Korean military organization was recommended.

Secretary of State George Catlett Marshall buried the *Wedemeyer Report.*

He ordered General Wedemeyer to step aside.

Marshall wrote Truman: *"I think this should be suppressed."*

The President's terse response was jotted on the letter: *"I agree -- H.T."*

Marshall was later accused of joining others in suppressing the *Wedemeyer Report.*

He boldly asserted: *"I did not join in suppression of the Report.*

"I personally suppressed it!"

Senator Joseph R. McCarthy wrote: *"If Marshall were merely stupid, the laws of probability would have dictated that at least some of his decisions would have served this country's interests."*

None of Marshall's decisions ever did!

Dean Acheson further baited the North Korean Communists when he became Truman's Secretary of State in 1949.

He announced to the world that the United States wouldn't defend South Korea!

It was considered to be outside of *"our defense perimeter."*

This was an engraved invitation for the North Korean Reds!

South Korea was deliberately left undefended in order to invite a military attack from the North!

And attack the Communists did!

Everything went exactly as anticipated by Marshall, Acheson, Truman and their fellow subversives.

Were all these men merely ignorant?

Not hardly!

In June of 1950, the United States became involved in its first *"no-win"* war.

A war of planned humiliation and demoralization.

Truman kept telling the American people: *"We are not at war."*

It was he said merely *"a police action"* against a *"bunch of North Korean bandits."*

The President knew better!

So did each and every one of his leftist advisors!

General of the Army Douglas MacArthur's forces were not allowed to chase attacking Russian MIGs back across the Yalu River!

Nor could they fire on anti-aircraft guns clearly in view on the other side!

MacArthur was ordered to ignore air fields and munitions dumps across the river!

And only the Korean half of the bridges spanning the Yalu River could be destroyed!

MacArthur charged: *"I realized for the first time that I had actually been denied the use of my full military power to safeguard the lives of my soldiers and the safety of my army.*

"It left me with a sense of inexpressible shock."

Vietnam a decade later was an instant replay of Korea!

USAF Lieutenant General Albert Stratemeyer recalled that the U.S. *"had sufficient air, bombardment, fighters, and reconnaissance so that I could have taken out those supplies, those airdromes on the other side of the Yalu.*

"I could have stopped that railroad operating and the people of China that were fighting could not have been supplied.

"But we weren't permitted to do it.

"As a result, a lot of American blood was spilled over there in Korea."

Thanks to the machinations of the traitorous Truman-Acheson duo, more than 50 thousand Americans were unnecessarily killed.

Yes unnecessarily in the degrading, morale-breaking Korean War that America was *forbidden* to win!

Treason?

Unquestionably!

Joseph W. Martin Jr. House minority leader was furious!

He said: *"If we are not in Korea to win, then this Administration should be indicted for the murder of thousands of American boys."*

Martin was absolutely correct!

An identical charge would apply years later to Vietnam.

Yet many of the same perpetrators along with a passel of newer traitors all got off scot free.

Truman shamefully fired MacArthur!

America's premier military strategist was removed from his Korean command on April 11, 1951.

He was guilty of simply wanting victory!

Not defeat!

His brilliant leadership was threatening to reverse the criminal no-win policy coordinated by Communists imbedded throughout the State Department!

The UN!

And the USSR!

MacArthur almost won in Korea despite the intimate ties between Comrades in Moscow and Comrades in Washington!

Secondly, MacArthur's recall came shortly after he'd demanded that traitors in the State Department and elsewhere be ousted by Truman.

The General knew his military operation in Korea was being subverted!

Yes by arrogant well protected Communist and pro-Communist elements within the Administration.

These subversives did their job well!

According to Willard Edwards of the Chicago Tribune: *"Every message McArthur sent to Washington during the Korean War was leaked to Moscow!"*

Truman ignored the General's spy warnings!

He was still defensive over the recent scandals involving Kremlin espionage agents Harry Dexter White and Alger Hiss.

Charges of more Reds in his Administration according to General MacArthur caused Truman *"the deepest resentment."*

As unbelievable as it may sound the United States actually protected Communist

Occupied China from attack during the Korean War!

The Seventh fleet was sent over with orders to guard the Communist coastline!

America's friend and ally Chiang Kai-shek was stopped from invading Red China.

This incredible order was given at the time Red Chinese soldiers were killing American boys on the battlefield in Korea!

Chiang's soldiers on Formosa volunteered to help the American fighting men in Korea.

There were six hundred thousand well-trained fighting men on Formosa who were ready to go at a moments notice.

They were rejected!

Owen Lattimore's traitorous 1949 plan was obviously being put into practice!

This dangerous Kremlin mole had proposed in a secret 1949 memorandum to the State Department:  *"The thing to do is let South Korea fall, but not let it look as if we pushed it."*

Communist Russia was behind the Korean War!

Just as it was the war in Vietnam!

Despotic Nikita Khrushchev admitted that Joe Stalin had personally *"ordered North Korea to attack South Korea."*

The U.S. had recently been victorious over the most advanced nations in the world:

Germany

Japan

and Italy

A mere five years later the most powerful country on the face of the earth acted as it were handcuffed.

It couldn't even defeat tiny North Korea and backward Communist Occupied China!

The reason?

Kremlin moles imbedded throughout the anti-American United Nations were directing the war for our Communist enemy in Korea.

These same Comrades were also orchestrating America's side of the war.

Senator Joe McCarthy was prophetic when in 1952 he said: *"The war in Korea in only one of the stepping stones to Communist world conquest.*

"Another stepping stone will be Indochina."

There can be absolutely no further question about this tragedy.

The unwanted Communist invaders were handed absolute control of Korea by traitors in the United States Government.

Kyung Rai Kim, a religious editor in Seoul told of some of the typical inhuman atrocities committed by the barbaric homicidal conquerors: *"An evangelist was killed by the Communists.*

"The Red police stripped him naked, bound him, and put him in an empty water pool.

"It was 17 degrees below zero that day.

"They filled the pool solid.

"My friend froze to death in 30 minutes.

"A lady evangelist was tied between two horses.

"Then the horses were sent running in different directions.

"250 pastors were killed by the Communists on the same day in the same place.

"The Red police made holes through the pastors' hands with an ax and bound them with wire rope, and then they shot them.

"At Wong Dang church, Red soldiers burned 83 Christians to death with gasoline."

Aiding and abetting Communist Occupied Yugoslavia has been the policy of the State Department under every President from Kennedy to Reagan.

Yugoslavian dictator Josef Broz Tito was carefully trained in the Soviet Union.

He was then sent to Yugoslavia by Stalin.

No one except the Soviets knew who he really was or where he really came from.

No one outside of the USSR even knew if Tito was his real name!

Despite overwhelming evidence to the contrary, President Kennedy's State Department information officer in 1961 followed President Eisenhower's policy.

He declared: *"Yugoslavia has remained independent, and has not participated in policies or programs to bring about the overthrow or subversion of legitimate governments by world Communism."*

This was an outright lie!

One can only surmise where Lincoln White obtained his information!

It was after all no more than the official Communist line!

But then this is the same leftist who as State Department press officer in 1950 lied when responding to Senator Joe McCarthy's charges of Red infiltration.

White's heated words: *"We know of no Communist members in this department and if we find any they will be summarily dismissed!"*

White was dead wrong!

His answer was preposterous!

He was a liar!

There'd been hundreds of Communists found in the State Department.

And they were protected and promoted rather than fired!

Subversive Dean Rusk (CFR) became Kennedy's Secretary of State in 1961.

He ignored normal channels and personally waived security checks on *152* questionable State Department employees.

Security checks were also bypassed by Rusk on more than *600* other subversives.

They were hired under a *"blanket waiver"* from January 1961 to May 1962.

Security evaluator Otto Otepka questioned Rusk's alarming lack of security procedures.

Otepka held up *150* promotions and job applications of subversives.

Secretary of State Rusk was incensed!

He initiated a vendetta to get rid of Otepka.

Rusk's retaliated during the spring of 1963.

His actions made Watergate seem like a Sunday School picnic!

Otepka was harassed incessantly.

His office was burglarized!

It was illegally bugged!

His phone was tapped!

His safe was broken open!

He was placed under constant surveillance as if he was a criminal!

No Kremlin mole under investigation had ever been treated so shabbily!

Rusk had Otepka transferred from security in June of 1963!

He was denied access to his files.

These files contained damaging evidence on hundreds of subversives in high policy-making positions!

Otepka was charged with conduct *"unbecoming an officer of the Department of State."*

Rusk and Kremlin moles buried throughout the State Department were somehow able to force an FBI investigation of Otepka!

Word was leaked that Otepka was going to be prosecuted for high crimes under the *Espionage Act*!

Otepka had according to State Department leftists given classified information to the enemy!

And who was the enemy?

Kremlin spies?

No!

It was the Senate Internal Security Subcommittee!

Incredible?

Yes!

But true nonetheless

A concerted effort to destroy what little was still left of the State Department's security program was culminated.

How?

Rusk fired Otepka in November of 1963.

All this subterfuge was geared to destroy an anticommunist patriot.

A patriot who just five years earlier had been given the meritorious service award.

It was clearly designed to destroy a man described by his boss Scott McLeod as *"the best security evaluator in government today."*

Regarding Otepka's firing Senator Dodd, cited the law: *"The right of persons employed in the civil service to furnish information to either House of Congress or to any committee or member thereof, shall not be denied or interfered with."*

Yet not a thing was done to help Otto Otepka!

Dodd charged that the State Department *"by its action in the Otepka case, has in effect nullified this statute and issued a warning to all Government employees that cooperation with the established Committees of the Senate, if this cooperation involves testimony unpalatable at higher echelon, is a crime punishable by dismissal."*

He was absolutely correct in his summation.

Yet nothing was done to help Otto Otepka!

The Senate Internal Security Subcommittee issued a report on State Department security in December 1967.

Senator Strom Thurmond of South

Carolina declared: *"There are two issues of paramount importance.*

"The first is whether a government employee loyal to his country can furnish information confidentially to the appropriate congressional committees when he sees wrongdoing.

"The second . . . State was trying to hide a new policy of phasing out effective security procedures.

"The highest officials no longer believed in loyalty in employing personnel.

"Quite simply, Mr. Otepka and a small band of associates were in the way."

Yet nothing was done to help Otto Otepka!

Congressman John M. Ashbrook said In 1968: *"When you study the Otto Otepka matter, you are inclined to exclaim, No wonder we are losing!"*

During a Ford-Carter Presidential debate, Jimmy Carter pledged: *"I would never give up complete control of the Panama Canal.*

"I would not relinquish the practical control of the Panama Canal Zone anytime in the foreseeable future."

He blatantly lied!

Once Carter became President, the State Department moved heaven and earth to surrender the American Canal in Panama.

The recipient of this outlandish leftist ploy was Communist drug-pusher Omar Torrijos Herrera, a colleague of Fidel Castro!

Torrijos said that Panama *"might adopt the path of Ho Chi Minh to achieve national liberation"*.

He threatened to do this should the United States not willingly give up the Canal!

Torrijos commanded no army, navy or air force!

His entire population wasn't 20 percent of that found in New York City!

Yet State Department conspirators pretended to be afraid this preposterous little despot might actually wage war against the most powerful nation in the world!

State quashed information about the intimate ties between Fidel Castro and Torrijos!

Conspirators in the State Department were determined to give away the Canal at any cost!

The enormity of their role in this treasonous deed of September 6, 1977, can't be measured!

Even more stunning is the fact that not only did traitors in State authorize giving away America's Canal.

They also arranged by treaty to pay the Marxist regime around $2 billion to take it off America's hands!

Treason?

You bet it was!

Meldrim Thomson declared: *"I find it abhorrent to witness an American President rushing to surrender the sovereign territory of the United States."*

The former New Hampshire Governor was correct.

There was never a legal question as to who owned the Panama Canal!

Panama *didn't even exist* as a country when the original deed was made!

The United States created the Republic of Panama out of a province of Columbia.

The Panama Canal Zone was as American as Hawaii or Alaska.

` Dan Smoot explained: *"In our 1903*

agreement with Panama we bought the Zone for 10 million dollars and a guaranteed annuity of 250 thousand dollars.

"This annuity was not a rental fee!

"It was a guarantee of revenue to keep the Panamanian government alive.

"We acquired full ownership and sovereignty making the Canal Zone United States territory forever."

Panama's dictator was a leading member of the Communist People's Party!

Torrijos' family members were prominent Reds in Panama!

His parents founded a Communist cell in Veraquas Province!

Ambassador Henry J. Taylor revealed that Torrijos' *"minister of foreign affairs and minister of labor are Communists."*

Other key members of his government were all known Communists!

Included was Manuel Antonio Noriega who headed the G-2 secret police

The chief Canal treaty negotiator for Panama?

Romulo Escobar Bethancourt.

He was a close friend of Cuba's Red dictator Fidel Castro.

And he was a lifelong Communist Party member!

His American counterpart was Sol Linowitz.

Linowitz was a registered foreign agent of Communist Occupied Chile!

In no way could State's role in this subterfuge with the howling jackals who rule Panama not be considered treason!

Carter's simpering betrayal of America's interests in the vital Canal was so serious it should have led to his immediate impeachment!

But it didn't!

The treason is compounded considering that the President and all the other conspirators were privy to the above information!

State Department personnel deliberately ignored the damaging data.

They allowed the outrageous scam to continue.

Everyone involved should have been and still could be held accountable!

For what?

Their part in another horrendous sellout to Communist forces in this hemisphere!

All those responsible, including the President of the United States, should have been and still could be prosecuted for treason!

To allow these people to continue to go unpunished is a moral travesty!

State Department subversives boldly engineered the ousting of anti-Communist Anastasio Somoza in Nicaragua!

How was this done?

On December 27, 1978 Somoza was issued a warning by our mole impregnated State Department.

This went into effect at the precise time Nicaragua was reeling under attack!

And who was the attacker?

Invading Communist terrorist forces from Costa Rica!

Somoza was ordered to not go after the Communist terrorists in their Costa Rican *"sanctuary"*.

On June 15, 1979, the State Department enforced an arms embargo against this reliable American friend and ally!

No weapons or ammunition shipments would be allowed for West Point graduate Somoza's pro-American government!

Once again a most familiar pattern of treachery emerged!

Dangerous Kremlin moles deeply buried at all levels of the State Department were still in charge of running American foreign policy!

These anti-American traitors were deliberately allowing a Communist dictatorship to be installed in Nicaragua!

What the Sandinistas were was no well guarded secret!

The *Washington Post* reported more than a year before the Communist regime was placed in power: *"They would establish a revolutionary state.*

"The guerrillas left no doubt about their admiration for the Cuban revolution, whose influence is powerful within the movement."

Diplomatic recognition was hastily bestowed on the Red barbarians.

This took place only four days after the Communists were forcibly installed in Managua on July 24, 1979.

Kremlin agents imbedded in all levels of the State Department *knew* all about the notorious Thomas Borge.

He headed the dreaded secret police!

He was a convicted murderer!

And he was a Communist Comrade!

They *knew* that all of the Communist Sandinista leadership had been trained in:

Panama

Cuba

Libya

Czechoslovakia

and other Red dictatorships.

Yet the Carter Administration funneled *$119 million* in foreign aid to the Communist leadership immediately after the takeover!

The loss of Nicaragua *was not* the result of an internal rebellion.

Leftist propagandists would like us to believe this garbage!

It was totally external!

It was nothing more than a well organized Red invasion from Cuba, Panama and Costa Rica!

The undeniable fact is that subversives in the State Department had long planned to deliver Nicaragua into the hands of Communist Occupied Russia!

It's evident that the Kremlin mole dominated State Department itself was and certainly still is a serious risk to the security of America!

It's also evident that enemies of the United States are unquestionably in control of the foreign policy establishment!

It's like a baseball game with all the players on the same team!

Or more specifically with the American players on the Kremlin team!

This problem wasn't new!

 It's been there ever since President Franklin Roosevelt opened the gates to a tidal wave of subversives and subversion prior to World War II.

There's been a covert Communist malignance stealthily sapping the vitality of the Republic ever since.

Signs of this metastasizing disease are readily discernible in many federal agencies!

But most notably in the bowels of the State Department.

Nevertheless even the most outspoken of Congressional and Presidential candidates dare not bring up or even acknowledge State Department domination by moles in service to the Kremlin!

It isn't just difficult but probably impossible to rid the State Department of Communists!

No one dares initiate an investigation!

None dare to even call a traitor a traitor!

In fact, even 1988 Presidential candidate Pat Robertson had the audacity to go no further than to cautiously refer to notorious Soviet spy Alger Hiss of Harvard as simply a *"misguided young man."*

The Communist infested State Department continues to do as much as humanly possible to turn the United States into a toothless tiger!

The ultimate goal of the conspirators is to do to America what they did to:

China
Angola
Cuba
Rhodesia
Nicaragua
and the rest!

These traitors fully intend for the United States to ultimately become a giant communist dictatorship!

A slave labor monstrosity kept in line under the ever watchful eye of their pals.

Those dictatorial leftist thugs who are determined to rule with a fist all nations under what they call a New World Order!

Consider the warning of Thomas Jefferson: *"Single acts of tyranny may be ascribed to the accidental opinion of a day; but a series of oppressions, begun at a distinguished period, and pursued unalterably through every change of ministers, too plainly prove a deliberate, systematic plan of reducing us to slavery."*

Rowan Gaither was President of the subversive, Ford Foundation in 1953.

He boldly summed up the plan of the subversives in our government.

He said this: *"Most of us here were, at one time or another, active in the OSS, the State Department, or the European Economic Administration.*

"During those times, and without exception, we operated under directives issued by the White House, the substance of

which was to the effect that we should make every effort to so alter life in the United States as to make possible a comfortable merger with the Soviet Union.

"We are continuing to be guided by just such directives."

Epilogue

The record covering crucial episodes of the McCarthy era has been massively and deliberately distorted from the very beginning!

Conveniently forgotten or deliberately overlooked are the 78 hearings held between 1951 and 1952 by Senator William E. Jenner's (R-Indiana) Senate Internal Security Subcommittee (SISS); the House Committee On Internal Security; the House Un-American Activities Committee (HUAC) under the chairmanship of both Martin Dies (D-Texas) and Francis Walters (D-Pa); the Federal Bureau of Investigation (FBI) under the guidance of J. Edgar Hoover; and other investigating committees and individuals.

Out of all of these investigations one man was selected:

To be stopped!

To be destroyed!

To be made an example!

Why?

So that no one would ever again dare to initiate any investigations into the penetration of our government agencies by communist agents (spies) in the employ of the Soviet Union!

Yes!

An obscure Senator from Wisconsin was deliberately targeted for this purpose!

Joseph McCarthy's incredibly successful investigations panicked those on the political left.

Their reaction was shockingly quick!

Key data was been suppressed, denied and even widely falsified.

This took place in the media, all branches of government and many alleged scholars entrenched in the ivory towers of our institutions of higher learning!

Such misreporting and misrepresentation of the facts continues today.

Much of the misinformation we were (and still are today) so carefully spoon-fed about Senator Joseph McCarthy the man and his investigations was no more than an admixture of uncheckable blovations from deceased third parties and demonstratable falsehoods!

For example, how many innocent people were harmed by McCarthy's revelations?

The correct answer?

Not one!

No!

Not One!

McCarthy's most virulent critics have had more than a half century to produce the names of the hundreds of innocent people they claim were destroyed by the astounding revelations of the Senator from Wisconsin.

Yet those highly skilled propagandists in our media and government and institutions of higher learning have been unable to name even one innocent person they claim was destroyed after being falsely accused by McCarthy!

How many innocent people committed suicide as a result of McCarthy's exposure?

The correct answer?

Not one!

Not one suicide can be attributed to the investigations conducted by McCarthy!

No! Not one!

According to the obscene claims made the highly skilled propagandists in our media, government and scholars entranced in those ivory towers of our colleges and universities there were a rash of suicides with bodies falling constantly of the heads of pedestrians below on the streets of Manhattan!

Once again, McCarthy's most virulent critics have had more than 50 years to produce the names of the hundreds of innocent people they claim committed suicide because of the astounding revelations of the Senator from Wisconsin.

Yet those highly skilled propagandists in our media and government and institutions of higher learning have been unable to name even one innocent person they claim committed suicide after being falsely accused by McCarthy!

No!

Not one!

But there were two suicides on record during the McCarthy period!

Neither was the result of an innocent person who'd been ruined by McCarthy's revelations!

Both were subversives who'd been exposed by McCarthy!

Both were subversives who'd been positively indentified as Kremlin agents!

Lawrence Duggan had been operating in the State Department as a widely known Soviet spy!

He'd been called to testify before a Congressional investigating committee.

Duggan never made it!

He conveniently "fell" from a window high up in a Manhattan skyscraper!

Fell?

Probably not!

He was more than likely pushed from or tossed out of the window by an assassin in the employ of the Soviet Union!

Why?

To make certain he didn't fold under pressure and start naming other Kremlin moles.

Secondly there was the unexpected demise of Harry Dexter White.

This Soviet agent discovered that he was being investigated by J. Edgar Hoover of the FBI!

He died of a sudden heart attack!

Coincidence?

Not hardly!

Was White's death a suicide?

Yes or at least so claimed McCarthy's critics!

Again, not hardly!

Heart attacks can readily be induced with the proper use of certain medicines administered by a hired assassin in the employ of the Kremlin!

Why?

Simply to eliminate anyone who might panic and decide to turncoat and reveal the names of other spies secretly entrenched deeply in the bowels of every branch of our government.

To sum up, most fit into one of three categories:

Conscience lacking incurable liars!

Those with an axe to grind!

Individuals who simply do not know the facts!

**Has anything really changed?
You Decide!**

If you liked this book in the *None Dare Call It Treason* series then you'll probably also enjoy reading the others!

Gift copies of this book ordered at can be robertwpelton.com or amazon.com

Available Titles

None Dare Call It Treason Book 1
The Internal Security Farce!
5.5" x 8.5" 103 pages $4.95
Order from robertwpelton.com
or amazon.com

None Dare Call It Treason Book 2
Never Ending Subversion
In Government!
5.5" x 8.5" 97 pages $4.95
Order from robertwpelton.com
or amazon.com

None Dare Call It Treason Book 3
America's Subversive State Department
Bloated With Security Risks
5.5" x 8.5" 99 pages $4.95
Order from robertwpelton.com
or amazon.com

None Dare Call It Treason Book 4
America's Illustrious State Department!
It's Machiavellian Misdeeds!
5.5" x 8.5" 105 pages $4.95
Order from robertwpelton.com
or amazon.com

None Dare Call It Treason Book 5
Our Presidents A Major Security Threat!
5.5" x 8.5" 73 pages $4.95
Order from robertwpelton.com
or amazon.com

None Dare Call It Treason Book 6
Presidential Words & Deeds
&Blatant Lies!
5.5" x 8.5" 124 pages $4.95
Order from robertwpelton.com
or amazon.com

None Dare Call It Treason Book 7
Subversives Close To Our Presidents
5.5" x 8.5" 104 pages $4.95
Order from robertwpelton.com
or amazon.com

None Dare Call It Treason Book 8
Henry Kissinger
The Shadowy Untouchable Kremlin Spy!
5.5" x 8.5" 74 pages $4.95
Order from robertwpelton.com
or amazon.com

None Dare Call It Treason Book 9
Inexcusably Arming America's Enemies!
5.5" x 8.5" 102 pages $4.95
Order from robertwpelton.com
or amazon.com

None Dare Call It Treason Book 10
Inexcusably Financing America's Enemies!
5.5" x 8.5" 102 pages $4.95
Order from robertwpelton.com
or amazon.com

None Dare Call It Treason Book 11
Treasonous   Trade With & Aid To
Enemies Of Freedom!
5.5" x 8.5" 91 pages $4.95
Order from robertwpelton.com
or amazon.com

None Dare Call It Treason Book 12
*Wholesale Treason During the War
In Vietnam!*
5.5" x 8.5" 120 pages $4.95
Order from robertwpelton.com
or amazon.com

None Dare Call It Treason Book 13
*Big Business
& Astounding Acts Of Treason!*
5.5" x 8.5" 95 pages $4.95
Order from robertwpelton.com
or amazon.com

None Dare Call It Treason Book 14
Illegally Importing Slave Made Goodies!
5.5" x 8.5" 91 pages $4.95
Order from robertwpelton.com
or amazon.com

None Dare Call It Treason Book 15
*The House That Hiss Built
The Anti-American United Nations!*
5.5" x 8.5" 117 pages $4.95
Order from robertwpelton.com
or amazon.com

None Dare Call It Treason Book 16
Security Risks in the House and Senate!
5.5" x 8.5" 62 pages $4.95
Order from robertwpelton.com
or amazon.com

None Dare Call It Treason Book 17
The Supreme Court A Devastating
Threat To National Security!
5.5" x 8.5" 98 pages $4.95
Order from robertwpelton.com
or amazon.com

Orders for Resale
40% Off Retail Price

Send Purchase Order to

christianamerica2@yahoo.com

MEET
THE AUTHOR

Robert W. Pelton has been writing and lecturing for more than 45 years on political and historical subjects.

He has published more than 100 books.

Mr. Pelton proudly claims a heritage going all the way back to well before the War for American Independence.

One of his ancestors, John Rogers, came to America on the Mayflower and was one of 41 signers of the Mayflower Compact.

Another, John Smith was one of the founders of Jamestown.

Peleg Pelton served as the fifer in the Continental Army at age 17 during the Battle of Saratoga (1777) and again in Yorktown (1781).

Captain Peter Hager was Commander of the Old Stone Fort in Schoharie, New York, 1780.

Another, Captain Bezaleel Tyler fought in the only Revolutionary War Battle taking place in Sullivan County, New York.

Mr. Pelton is a member of Sons of the Revolution (SOR), and Sons of the American Revolution (SAR).

Pelton may be contacted at: christianamerica2@yahoo.com